THE HOWARDS
OF NORFOLK

A fascinating album of the lives and times of leading members of the Howard family of Norfolk, the head of which is Premier Duke and Earl Marshal of England. Some of the fascinating characters described are Lord Howard of Effingham, who with Drake repelled the Armada; the Earl of Surrey, the Elizabethan poet and courtier; and two of Henry VIII's queens, Anne Boleyn and her cousin Catherine Howard.

The book is fully illustrated with portraits and contemporary prints, together with pictures of Arundel Castle, ancestral home of the Howards.

SOLA VIRTUS INVICTA

Achievement of Arms of the Duke of Norfolk

THE HOWARDS
OF NORFOLK

by Neil Grant

Illustrated with photographs and contemporary prints

FRANKLIN WATTS
London and New York

© 1972 Franklin Watts Limited, 8 Cork Street, London, W.1
Revised and reprinted 1979
SBN 85166 236 6

The Publisher wishes to express great appreciation to His
Grace The Duke of Norfolk for kind permission to reproduce
illustrations as follows: pages 10, 17, 18, 20, 26, 38, 40, 46, 47,
49, 51, 56, 57, 58, 60, 61, 65, 66, 67, 68, 71 (top), 76, 77, 78,
79, 83, 84, 86, 91. Grateful thanks are also due to Mr. R. W.
Puttock, Castle Manager at Arundel Castle, for all his help in
connection with this book.

The Publisher also wishes to thank the following for permission
to reproduce the following photographs: Radio Times Hulton
Picture Library, page 9, 12, 13 (bottom), 21, 22 (bottom), 32,
72 (top), 73; National Portrait Gallery, pages 11 (bottom),
13 (top), 15, 19, 28, 33, 34, 45 (bottom), 48, 52, 54, 55, 66, 70,
73 (bottom), 82; Mansell Collection, pages 8, 22 (top), 24, 27,
29, 30, 31, 37, 50, 53, 63, 69, 71 (bottom), 80, 81, 87, 88;
Camera Press, page 39; Aerofilms Limited, page 64; Ashmolean
Museum, page 59; Eastern Daily Press, page 89; Richard Burn,
page 7; Brighton Evening Argus, page 92; British Tourist
Authority, page 14; Central Public Library, Norwich, pages 42,
43, 75; Controller of Her Majesty's Stationery Office (Crown
Copyright Reserved), page 36. P. K. Inch, page 11. Foto Felici,
Rome, page 93.
Jacket by Dorothy H. Ralphs.

First published 1972 by Franklin Watts Limited.
Filmset and printed in Great Britain by
BAS Printers Limited, Over Wallop, Hampshire

Contents

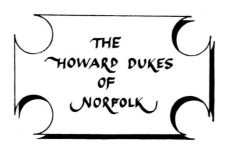

THE HOWARD DUKES OF NORFOLK

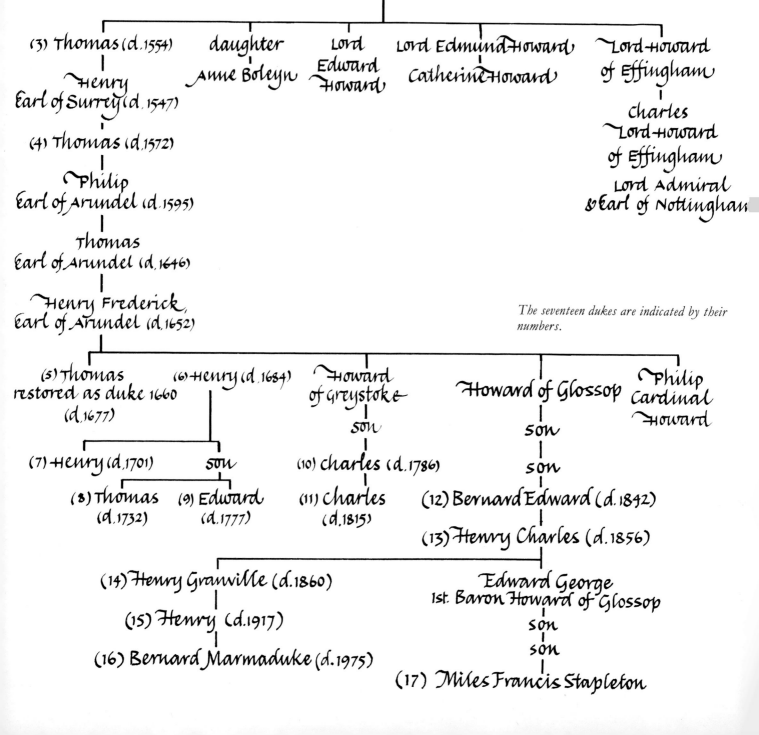

Sir Robert Howard (d.1436) — Lady Margaret Mowbray

(1) John (killed & attainted 1485)

(2) Thomas (d.1524)

(3) Thomas (d.1554)   daughter   Lord   Lord Edmund Howard   Lord Howard
     Anne Boleyn   Edward   Catherine Howard   of Effingham
     Howard

Henry
Earl of Surrey (d.1547)
                                       charles
                                       Lord Howard
(4) Thomas (d.1572)   of Effingham

Philip   Lord Admiral
Earl of Arundel (d.1595)   & Earl of Nottingham

Thomas
Earl of Arundel (d.1646)

Henry Frederick,
Earl of Arundel (d.1652)   *The seventeen dukes are indicated by their*
                                               numbers.

(5) Thomas   (6) Henry (d.1684)   Howard   Howard of Glossop   Philip
restored as duke 1660   of Greystoke   Cardinal
(d.1677)   son   son   Howard

(7) Henry (d.1701)   son   (10) charles (d.1786)   son

   (8) Thomas   (9) Edward   (11) charles   (12) Bernard Edward (d.1842)
     (d.1732)   (d.1777)   (d.1815)

                                          (13) Henry Charles (d.1856)

(14) Henry Granville (d.1860)   Edward George
                                    1st. Baron Howard of Glossop

(15) Henry (d.1917)   son

(16) Bernard Marmaduke (d.1975)   son

                               (17) Miles Francis Stapleton

The Rise of the Howards

The present Duke of Norfolk, Miles Francis Stapleton Fitzalan-Howard, is the seventeenth member of the Howard family to hold the title. He is the premier duke of England: his name stands higher on the list of English nobility than all except royal dukes, like the Duke of Gloucester or the Duke of Kent. Although some earldoms are older, Norfolk is the oldest dukedom in England, and the present duke is descended almost directly from the first Howard Duke of Norfolk, who died in 1485.

As the old rhyme says:

"When Adam delved and Eve span,
Who was then the gentleman?"

Even the oldest families must start somewhere, for there were no earls or dukes when the inhabitants of the British Isles lived in caves. The Howards can trace their ancestors back further than most families. But there comes a time when the line fades out and facts grow vague. One story says that the name Howard was once the same as Hereward, and that the Dukes of Norfolk are descended from that old Anglo-Saxon hero Hereward the Wake, who defended his stronghold in the fens of East Anglia from the conquering Normans of 1066.

The first Howard ancestor whom we can really be sure about is Sir William Howard, whose portrait appears in one of the stained-glass windows of the church of Long Melford, in Suffolk.

(a) *Norfolk, showing place names in the Howard story.*

(b) *Sir William Howard's portrait in stained glass in Long Melford Church.*

7

Seal of Edward I, both sides

Sir William came from the village of East Winch, in West Norfolk, which is therefore the oldest known home of the Howards. Today, rumbling lorries pass through the village carrying sugar beet to the nearby factory in King's Lynn, and nothing is left of Sir William's old manor house. But the arms of the Howards can still be seen carved on the font of the little church of All Saints.

Sir William was a lawyer, and a good one. He came to the notice of King Edward I and, before he died, he had risen to be Chief Justice of the Court of Common Pleas, a high office for a man who had no influence at the king's court. He was a clever businessman too and built up a large estate near King's Lynn, partly through buying land and partly through marriage: he had two wives and both brought him property.

Sir William died in about 1308, but his son, Sir John Howard, followed his father's sensible example and expanded his property by marrying a rich wife. Lady Joan was, in fact, related to the royal family, and the manors that she owned made her husband the greatest landowner in West Norfolk and lord of Castle Rising (the castle still stands, a splendid ruin, above the village cricket ground).

The lands and influence of the Howards continued to grow. The second Sir John Howard was appointed Admiral of the North Seas, the first of many Howard admirals. His grandson, the third Sir John, died in the Middle East on a crusade when he was over seventy. But the most important event for the future greatness of the family was the marriage, which took place in about 1420, between Sir Robert Howard and Lady Margaret Mowbray.

Lady Margaret was the eldest daughter of Thomas Mowbray, first Duke of Norfolk in the Mowbray line (he appears in the first act of Shakespeare's play *Richard II*). After the king and the royal family, the Mowbray Duke of Norfolk was the greatest man in the kingdom; but his line was soon to die out. Much of the Mowbray inheritance would pass, through Lady Margaret, into the hands of the Howards.

8

Yet at this time the Howard fortunes received their first serious check. In one way or another, most of the Norfolk estates built up by old Sir William and his successors had been lost: in 1460, when Sir John Howard (son of Sir Robert and Lady Margaret Mowbray) was hoping to be appointed a knight of the shire, he was opposed by some people on the grounds that he did not own sufficient lands there. After 150 years of growth, it seemed that the Howards had been halted. Yet it was this same Sir John Howard who became the first Duke of Norfolk in the Howard line.

Castle Rising—a splendid example of a Norman castle.

Jack of Norfolk

John Howard, the future first duke, was born in about 1421 and succeeded to the Howard estates at the age of eighteen. He had no brothers, and the survival of the Howard name depended on him alone. No one could have thought that the Howards' chances of survival were good, because John Howard was living in a warlike age when the knights and barons of England were being killed off at an alarming rate.

Like all the Howards since Sir William, the founder of the family, John Howard was a soldier, and spent most of his life on active service. At the age of thirty, while taking part in the siege of a town in France, he was wounded and taken prisoner. But some friend or relative must have paid the ransom that his captors demanded, for within two years he was back in England.

England in the mid-fifteenth century was no safer than France, for the country was involved in the long struggle called the Wars of the Roses. The reason for these wars was the claim of two branches of the royal family (the House of York and the House of Lancaster) for the throne. Most of the chief barons and earls fought on one side or another—and often switched from York to Lancaster and back again as it suited them. The Howards, however, remained faithful to the House of York. Backed by his powerful Mowbray relations, John Howard upheld the Yorkist cause in Norfolk.

Sometimes the conflict was carried on by peaceful means: Howard was one of the representatives in parliament who compelled the Lancastrian king, Henry VI, to make the Duke of York his heir. But often the argument ended in war. In 1461 Howard gave a good account of himself at the Battle of Towton—a decisive victory for the Yorkists. This battle brought him to the attention of the Yorkist leader, Edward IV, and it also caused the deaths of several enemies of the Howards, including the Earl of Oxford whose forbears had got hold of some of the Howard estates.

Although John Howard did not immediately regain the old family lands, his influence at court began to rise sharply. When Edward IV became king after the Battle of Towton, Howard was

The cross commemorating the Battle of Towton.

Henry VI

appointed King's Carver. This office did not mean that Howard in person had to carve the joint at dinner time; but it gave him a place in the king's household, where he could whisper suggestions into the royal ear. Edward also made him Sheriff of Norfolk and Suffolk and gave him the charge of several castles in East Anglia. After the Mowbrays, the Howards were the greatest family in that part of the country.

For the next few years, Howard led the life of a powerful English baron. He was the king's chief lieutenant in East Anglia; he attended the royal court and took part in tournaments, where his skill in the joust made him a popular figure. He was a particular friend of the king's brother, Richard, Duke of Gloucester (the future Richard III). The great keep of Norwich Castle sometimes echoed with the shouts and laughter of Howard and Gloucester as they enjoyed themselves at a boisterous feast after a hard day inspecting the defences.

View of Norwich Castle and part of the city of Norwich.

John Howard seems to have been a man of average height, with a strong, square face, a nose that looked as though it had been broken in one of its owner's many fights, and a moustache but no beard—a style that was then becoming old-fashioned. From what we can tell about his character, he was less selfish and more loyal than most men of his class and time.

His duties as a servant of the king took him all over Britain and to the continent. He fought in the north of England against a Lancastrian invasion; he subdued a rebellion in Wales, and he acted as ambassador between the kings of England and France. One of his most famous exploits took place in 1470, after Edward IV had been defeated and turned off the throne. The king was kept a prisoner in a castle in Yorkshire, but he was not well guarded and Howard, together with Sir William Stanley and other Yorkist leaders, succeeded in rescuing him from captivity. They rode fast to King's Lynn, then quite a large port, where Howard had ships waiting. Under Howard's protection, Edward escaped to Holland.

A year later, Edward returned, gathered an army in Yorkshire and marched south. Howard set up the king's standard in East Anglia, and joined the king on his march towards Barnet Heath where, on the morning of Easter Sunday, one of the bloodiest battles of the Wars of the Roses ended in victory for the Yorkists. Howard's eldest son Thomas (later the second Duke of Norfolk) was badly wounded in the fighting.

A few years after that, Howard was in France with the king, this time exercising his powers of diplomacy. One evening, after the two kings of England and France had reached agreement (assisted by the menacing appearance of several thousand English soldiers), Howard came to the French king and whispered in his ear the suggestion that he should fetch Edward to Paris, where the two monarchs might celebrate their agreement and enjoy "a right merry time" together. Poor King Louis' heart sank, for he had heard stories of King Edward's "merry times". Yet he could hardly refuse. So he smiled a little desperately and said what a splendid idea it was—but, he added, unfortunately he could not

Edward IV

The Battle of Barnet, from a manuscript.

13

spare the time as he was about to start a war with his neighbour, the Duke of Burgundy.

Back in England, Howard heard that the last Mowbray Duke of Norfolk had recently died, leaving a little girl as his only heir. She also died not long afterwards and the huge Mowbray estates were split up. The largest portion passed into the possession of that fortunate courtier, the Lord Howard.

In 1483 King Edward died. He was only 41 years old and his two sons were young children. Howard's friend, Richard of Gloucester, ruled as Lord Protector for his nephew, while the young King Edward V and his brother disappeared into the Tower of London. The Tower was a royal residence as well as a prison but—prison or home—the two young princes were never seen again outside its steep and stony walls. Richard of Gloucester, although some people suspected him of murdering the princes, was crowned as King Richard III.

The Tower of London

One of the first acts of the new king was to raise his old friend the Lord Howard to the vacant titles of Duke of Norfolk and Earl Marshal of England (the present Duke is also Earl Marshal, as his ancestors have been since the seventeenth century). Nowadays, the Earl Marshal is mostly concerned with royal ceremonies, but in earlier times it was also a military rank: the Earl Marshal commanded the soldiers of the king's household.

Richard III

The new Duke, besides his other honours, also held the post of Lord High Steward, and at Richard's coronation he walked in front of the king carrying the crown. His son and heir, who had been created Earl of Surrey (another title that has continued in the family to the present), carried the sword of state.

But Richard III, the last Yorkist king, was not to reign for long. In August, 1485, just two years after the coronation, a young man called Henry Tudor landed in Wales and began to gather an army. His claim to the throne was not a very good one, but then Richard himself had gained the crown in suspicious circumstances and, in the unsettled state of England, there were always men willing to join a rebellion against the king.

Lancastrian supporters flocked to the banner of Henry Tudor, while the Duke of Norfolk began to collect his forces to support King Richard. Some of the king's enemies tried to persuade him to change sides, but the chief of the Howards remained faithful to the king. Others were not so loyal. Unknown to Norfolk or the king, the powerful Lord Stanley, for one, was secretly in touch with Henry Tudor. The smell of treachery was in the air. Someone pinned a warning on the Duke of Norfolk's gates:

"Jack of Norfolk, be not too bold,
For Dickon thy master is bought and sold."

Norfolk and Surrey met the king at Leicester and held a council of war in the "Blue Boar". Norfolk was to command the vanguard, with Surrey as his lieutenant. Lord Stanley was to take his place on the flank of Richard's army. And so they moved to confront the invader, on Bosworth field.

Helmets were buckled on, bows tested and arrows trimmed. Trumpets sounded, and the armies advanced towards each other.

Suddenly, above the clatter of armour and horses, the air thrummed with the flights of arrows. Minutes later, the armies clashed and the solid ranks of men were split up into dozens of desperately struggling groups.

At first the fiercest fighting was between the two vanguards: Norfolk for King Richard, and the Earl of Oxford—an old rival of the Howards—for Henry Tudor. For all his sixty-odd years, "Jack of Norfolk" fought as vigorously as any.

Then Stanley struck. At a pre-arranged signal, he swung his large force over to Henry's side and, sweeping down between the vanguard and the main army, attacked Norfolk in the rear. The situation became desperate for the royal forces. Amid the confusion, Norfolk sighted his opponent, Oxford, and spurred his horse towards him. Oxford charged to meet him and with a single crash their lances splintered against each other's armour. Drawing their heavy swords, they circled around, each man aiming great scything chops at his opponent. Norfolk wounded Oxford in the left arm, but Oxford retaliated and, swinging at Norfolk's head, he hacked off the face-guard of his helmet. Seeing his enemy unprotected, Oxford chivalrously held back, but at that moment an arrow came winging out of the crowd and struck Norfolk in the face. With a great crash, the first Duke of Norfolk fell dead upon the field of Bosworth.

Seeing his father fall, Surrey charged recklessly into attack. Swiftly surrounded, he fought bravely and cut off one man's arm with a single stroke of his sword. At last he fell wounded and, handing his sword to an opponent, Sir Gilbert Talbot, he asked to be killed so that he might not be taken prisoner. But Talbot, admiring the courage of the young earl, refused, and ordered his men to carry the wounded man carefully from the battlefield.

In another part of the field, King Richard died fighting like a tiger: Henry Tudor won the crown and became King Henry VII of England.

The estates of the Howards were confiscated by an act of parliament. The duke was dead and Surrey, in prison, had lost his title and was in danger of execution as a traitor. The House of Howard seemed to be doomed to disappear.

After the battle of Bosworth, Thomas, Earl of Surrey, son of the first Duke of Norfolk, stands before Henry VII and defends his allegiance to Richard III— an early nineteenth century painting at Arundel Castle.

In 1485 Thomas Howard, late Earl of Surrey, lay in prison recovering from his wounds, a landless outlaw expecting a death sentence. But the new king, Henry VII, was not a cruel man, and the friends—and former enemies—of the Howard family combined to persuade the king to spare Howard's life. All the same, he remained in prison for over three years.

Henry VII

He regained his freedom and the title "Earl of Surrey" (but not his lands and dukedom), because King Henry needed a good general to help put down a rebellion in the north, which was supported by King James IV of Scotland. The Earl was ready to serve the Tudor king as loyally as his father had served Richard III, and he was a soldier of proved ability. When King Henry was on his deathbed he ordered all the Howard lands to be returned to their rightful owner, but it was not until 1514, only ten years before his own death, that Surrey was restored to the title "Duke of Norfolk".

Like most great nobles of his time, Surrey was a soldier before everything. As a politician he was too simple and straightforward a man to be truly successful in the devious diplomacy of the sixteenth century. He was a man of great courage and pride, but his pride was not the showy kind. At a time when most great men treated ordinary people no better than dogs, he was liked and respected by his people in East Anglia.

Taking up his post of king's lieutenant in the north, Surrey swiftly suppressed the rebels and advanced against the King of Scots. He captured Ayton castle and knocked down its defences. King James IV then suggested that they should fight a duel, man to man, but Surrey refused, saying his job was to do as much damage to the Scots as he could, and fighting King James, whether he won or lost, would not make much difference. The Scottish king was fearful of risking his army against Surrey and withdrew to safety. After reinforcing the castles along the Scottish border, Surrey also disbanded his men.

His second meeting with the Scots king was happier. Margaret, daughter of Henry VII, was to marry James as part of an effort to preserve peace between the two kingdoms, and

This sword which hangs at Arundel Castle, was taken from James IV of Scotland after his defeat at Flodden.

Surrey was appointed to escort the bride to Edinburgh. At the wedding ceremony, he gave the bride away on behalf of the English king; but the peace did not last long.

Howard and Stewart were to have yet one more meeting, in 1513, eleven years after the royal wedding. That meeting is commemorated in history books by the famous name of Flodden.

The young king, Henry VIII, eager to cut a dash as a man of war, had led an expedition across the Channel to France in an attempt to revive the English claim to the French throne. As an experienced general, Surrey might have been expected to go too, but he was left behind—perhaps on the advice of Thomas Wolsey, the man who was soon to become the king's chief minister.

As things turned out, it was fortunate that a commander of Surrey's experience remained in England. James of Scotland, taking advantage of the English king's absence, crossed the border with an army of 30,000 men. Surrey, with an army only two-thirds the size, hastened to meet him.

The Scots were drawn up in a powerful position on Flodden Edge, commanding the plain. But Surrey managed to turn the enemy's flank and compelled the Scots to leave their strong position. The fighting was ferocious. The English cavalry, under Lord Dacre, drove back the left wing of the Scots, and another Scots division was broken up by Lord Thomas Howard (later third Duke of Norfolk). The long spears carried by the Scots infantry were clumsy weapons, and the shorter, hooked spears, called bills, of the English soldiers proved more deadly. King James himself fell only a few feet away from Surrey and ten thousand of his men, including many nobles and officers of state, fell with him.

Flodden was a famous victory. It revenged England's defeat by the Scots at Bannockburn a hundred years before, and it ended the menace of a Scottish invasion of northern England for many years. King Henry's campaign in France produced no such spectacular success, and the Earl of Surrey was the toast of England. The king, pleased if a little jealous, restored his titles of Duke of Norfolk and Earl Marshal.

20

Thereafter ensue the trewe encountre or Bataple lately don betwene Englāde and Scotlande. In whiche bataple the Scottsshe Kynge was slayne.

The maner of thaduaūcesynge of my lord of Surrey tresourier and Marshall of Englande and leuetenāte generall of the north pties of the same with xxvi M men to wardes the kynge of Scottz and his Armye vewed and noūbred to an hundred thousande men at the leest.

Emperor Charles V

But the victorious duke did not play such a large part in affairs of state after Flodden as his glowing prestige suggested. The crafty Wolsey, now a cardinal, was jealous of the power of the English nobility and made sure that men like Norfolk did not gain too much influence with the king.

Still, Norfolk was not idle. In 1517 he put down a revolt by the London apprentices, and afterwards persuaded the angry Henry not to treat the rebels harshly. Three years later, Henry left him in charge of the country while he made another visit—a peaceful one this time—to France. Norfolk was compelled to be polite and friendly towards the powerful Wolsey, and he even had to preside at the trial for treason of his friend, the Duke of Buckingham. Sickened by the execution of the duke, he left the court and vowed never to return.

He could not keep that vow. Henry insisted that men like Norfolk should attend him from time to time, if only to prove that they were not busy raising a rebellion against him. In 1522, the old duke was sent as an ambassador to the Holy Roman Emperor, Charles V, who honoured the House of Howard by giving the duke's eldest son the title of admiral of the imperial dominions.

Norfolk saw King Henry for the last time in the spring of 1523, when they had a long and friendly conversation. Afterwards he retired for good to the great castle of Framlingham, which had once been the seat of the Mowbray dukes of Norfolk and, before them, of the Bigods, Earls of Norfolk in Norman times. There he died, in 1524, when he was not far off eighty years of age.

Framlingham Castle, Suffolk.

Edward Howard, Lord Admiral

The second Duke of Norfolk was married twice and had at least fifteen children, most of them boys. As nearly all his sons in turn produced children of their own, the second duke is responsible for a very large number of branches in the Howard family tree. Some of his descendants we shall meet later: Charles, Lord Howard of Effingham, who commanded the English fleet against the Armada, was his grandson; Anne Boleyn and Catherine Howard, second and fifth wives of Henry VIII, were his granddaughters. Of his immediate descendants the most famous (and probably the most famous of all the Dukes of Norfolk) was his eldest son Thomas, who succeeded him. Yet as a young man, Thomas Howard was overshadowed by his dashing younger brother, Lord Edward.

Edward was the first of the Howards to win fame as a great admiral. He began his naval career very young: he was still in his teens when he first took part in a naval battle. He and his brother served under their father against the Scots, and Edward became a close friend of the young king Henry VIII.

His first victory at sea was against a well-known Scottish captain, Andrew Barton, whom he caught one day off the coast of England. According to an old ballad:

"Lord Howard he took sword in hand
And off he smote Sir Andrew's head."

More likely he simply made him a prisoner, but at any rate, the exploit was well-known enough to be celebrated in a song.

But the enemy that had most cause to curse the name of Howard the admiral was France. He chased French ships up and down the English Channel, often landing on the French coast to set fire to a town or attack a castle. He was energetic and courageous, but he was sometimes rash.

In August, 1512, Lord Edward Howard launched an attack on the French harbour of Brest. He had a fleet of 25 ships, in-

A sixteenth-century ship bearing the Howard arms.

cluding the *Regent*, whose captain was Sir Thomas Knyvett, his brother-in-law and close friend. The French were expecting the attack and their fleet intercepted the English off the coast. In those days, battles at sea were not much different from battles on land. The object was to get close to the enemy ship, hold it with grappling irons, then leap aboard and fight hand to hand. Knyvett's *Regent* bore down on the larger French flagship, and a fierce battle began. The French ship caught fire, and soon the *Regent* was blazing too, but Knyvett fought on among the flames. At last the fire reached the powder barrels, there was a terrific explosion, and both ships were destroyed. Not a man survived.

24

Enraged by the death of his friend, Howard furiously pursued the French and again led his men against the towns and villages of the French coast, burning and destroying. He vowed that he would not return to England until Sir Thomas Knyvett's death was avenged.

The next year (1513), having been appointed Lord Admiral of England, Howard renewed his attack on Brest. He had fewer ships this time, and the French fleet was in harbour, strongly defended by cannon on the shore. Yet Lord Edward, with his usual reckless courage, decided to attack at once. Under heavy fire, he approached the French admiral's flagship, and with about twenty men behind him, he scrambled on board and began to lay about him. But the ropes which fastened his boat to the French flagship broke, and together with the handful who had leapt on board alongside him, he was cut off from reinforcements. If he had told the French who he was, he could have saved his life, but he did not do so. Hopelessly outnumbered and bleeding from many wounds, he was slowly forced back by the French soldiers. At the last, he tore off the golden whistle that he wore around his neck—the only sign of his rank as admiral —and threw it into the sea. A minute later he was forced to jump into the water himself, but, weakened by loss of blood, he drowned in the strong currents of the bay. He was about 35 years old.

The Third Duke

Thomas Howard, the third duke, is the best-known of all the Howard Dukes of Norfolk. When he succeeded to his father's title in 1524, he was already a man of fifty with a long career as a soldier and courtier which stretched back to the days when he was a page boy at the court of King Henry VII. He had married a royal princess (though she died young and he married again); he served under his father in Scotland in 1497 and fought with his brother Edward against the Scots captain Andrew Barton in 1511. He led an expedition (not very successfully) to Spain and fought at Flodden. He followed his younger brother as Lord Admiral of England. Perhaps as a result of his quarrel with Cardinal Wolsey, he was sent to Ireland, where he served for two years as King Henry's viceroy and managed to enforce English rule on the fiery Irish chieftains. As Lord Admiral, he led a fleet against France and later took command of the English army in Normandy. In 1523 he was recalled to command again against the Scots, who were once more looking dangerous. He drove out the anti-English Scots leader and strengthened English influence in Scotland.

So, by the time he became Duke of Norfolk, he was not only the most powerful noble in England, he was also the most experienced soldier and politician. He was close to the centre of affairs in the court and the country throughout the reign of Henry VIII and outlived the king by seven years. That alone was no small achievement, for there was a high casualty rate among the ministers of Henry, especially in his later years when the king saw treason lurking in every corner.

The third Duke of Norfolk is not, to us, a very attractive character. The qualities needed to survive at the court of King Henry VIII were not pleasant ones. Ruthlessness, skill at lying and devotion to self-interest were required, and Norfolk, though not so clever a politician as Wolsey or Thomas Cromwell, learned early in life that loyalty and honesty could be more dangerous than desirable. The first necessity was to keep the favour of the king—by any means available.

That was a fact that his enemy Wolsey knew as well as any-one. When the king decided that he wanted a divorce from his

Cardinal Wolsey

27

first wife, Catherine of Aragon, Wolsey knew that, difficult though the task might prove, the divorce, which only the pope could grant, had to be obtained.

Why did Henry want a divorce? In the first place, he had no son to succeed him, and Catherine had passed the age of child-bearing. And in the second place, Henry had fallen in love with Anne Boleyn, a niece of the Duke of Norfolk, and wanted to make her his queen. Norfolk naturally supported Henry's wish for a divorce, and on the quiet he coached his niece in how to handle her difficult lover.

Anne Boleyn, second wife of Henry VIII, mother of Queen Elizabeth I.

Despite Wolsey's best efforts, the pope delayed giving a judgement in Henry's favour and in the end the king lost patience. Wolsey had failed, and Henry would get his divorce by other means. The new religion of Protestantism was spreading rapidly on the continent, and plenty of people in England encouraged Henry to break away from the pope and the Church of Rome. The result was that England ceased to be a Roman Catholic country: it was still Catholic in religion, but headed by the king instead of the pope. Cardinal Wolsey, the Ipswich butcher's son who had risen to be the greatest man in the kingdom, fell from power with a spectacular crash and died soon afterwards. Anne Boleyn became Queen of England.

But the triumph of the Howards was short. Anne Boleyn had no sooner reached the throne than she forgot her family "duty" and stopped listening to the advice of her uncle. Anyway, having at last got Anne as his wife, the king began to lose interest in her and she, like her predecessor, failed to provide Henry with a son (though she had a daughter, the future Queen Elizabeth I). Norfolk had expected to step into Wolsey's shoes as the king's chief adviser, but found that he was superseded by Thomas Cromwell. Furious at what he regarded as Anne's treachery and at Cromwell's influence with the king, Norfolk began to plot against them both. When Anne was tried for adultery, on feeble enough evidence, it was her uncle who presided over her trial. Neither Norfolk nor the king showed much regret when the foolish and unlucky Anne lost her head on the execution block on Tower Hill.

Strangely, the Duke of Norfolk suffered from marriage problems rather like those that Henry VIII had with Catherine of Aragon. The Duchess of Norfolk (she was his second wife, the first having died young) did not get on at all well with her husband and, although they did not separate completely until 1534, they had been quarrelling for many years before that. Although it was no doubt a serious matter for both parties at the time, the squabble between the duke and duchess has its funny side from our distance of 450 years. The duchess could write letters that

The block and the axe at the Tower of London.

almost steam with anger at her husband, who had taken up with a woman called Bess Holland, the daughter of his steward. The duchess made no secret of her wrongs and, to keep her quiet, the duke confined her to the new mansion he had built at Kenninghall in Norfolk (Framlingham castle was too grim and uncomfortable a home for a Tudor courtier like Norfolk). He even took away her clothes and jewels to prevent her escaping.

The duchess bombarded Cromwell with complaints of "my husband's crafty ways" and "that harlot [she meant Bess Holland] which has put me to all this trouble". She swore that Norfolk had dragged her round the room by the hair and given her "a wound in the head". Norfolk retorted just as angrily that he had done nothing of the sort. Eventually, she retired to a house in Hertford-shire with an allowance—too small, according to the duchess—from her husband. Bess Holland ruled the roost at Kenninghall.

Having begun his attack on the power of the Church, King Henry VIII found it difficult to stop. Encouraged by Cromwell, Protestant influence was increasing. The king was short of money (kings usually were in those days) and he was easily persuaded that the huge estates of the Church, especially the great abbeys and monasteries, scattered throughout England, ought to be confiscated by the Crown.

The dissolution of the monasteries, while it solved the king's financial problems for a short time, caused much disturbance. Many people, already shocked by the growth of Protestantism, were angered by the sacking of these ancient religious houses. In the north a rebellion broke out, called the Pilgrimage of Grace. The pilgrims wanted to stop the attacks on the old religion and to prevent any more Church property being seized. They resented the interference of the government in their lives, and they wanted to get rid of men like Cromwell. But they insisted that they were loyal to the king. Unfortunately for them, they believed that the king would then be loyal to them.

In this crisis Henry called on Norfolk, his ablest general. It had all happened so fast that Norfolk at first confronted the rebels with only a handful of men; but, while talks went on, his army

Thomas Cromwell

Syon House, a dissolved religious house; later, Catherine Howard was imprisoned there.

was gathering. Many meetings and discussions took place, and Norfolk and the king promised that some at least of the rebels' demands would be satisfied. They also promised that no one would be prosecuted for taking part in the rebellion. With this assurance, the pilgrims disbanded.

Later, a few more riots broke out in isolated places, and the king used them as an excuse to break his promises. Norfolk began a campaign of terror in Yorkshire. The leaders of the rising were swiftly executed (some by the horrible method of hanging, drawing and quartering) and Norfolk's men rode through the towns and villages burning houses and hanging men and women without trial.

Having completed the king's bloody revenge on those who had dared to rise against him, Norfolk retired for a time to Kenninghall and the comforts provided by Bess Holland. Despite his actions against the pilgrims, Norfolk was a strong Catholic (as most of his successors have been). He had no liking for the new religion, which seemed to be growing stronger every day. Even stronger was his hatred for the king's chief minister, Thomas Cromwell. Their long struggle, often carried on behind a mask of friendship, was drawing to a head. Norfolk had thought of a scheme that would finish Cromwell and make the Howard family supreme at Henry VIII's court.

The Pilgrimage of Grace

Catherine Howard

A portrait thought until recently to be that of Catherine Howard, Henry VIII's fifth wife.

Henry VIII

Henry VIII's marriage to Anne of Cleves, his fourth wife, had been arranged by Thomas Cromwell, who considered that the Protestant Duchy of Cleves would make a useful ally for England. The king had not met his bride until she arrived in England for the wedding, but he had heard that she was beautiful and had been shown a flattering portrait of her. Unfortunately, the lady did not measure up to these glowing reports, and Henry felt that he been engaged to a frump. Nor was Anne very eager to become the wife of Henry of England, who had lost the good looks of his youth and, as a marriage partner, was beginning to seem rather dangerous. Anne of Cleves was soon shunted off into a quiet country house, and a divorce was obtained from Cranmer, the archbishop of Canterbury.

Cromwell's error in choosing Anne of Cleves as a wife was a fatal one. He slipped from the king's high favour and, once he had begun to slip, his slide could not be halted. As Cromwell's influence declined, Norfolk's rose, and the duke vengefully hounded his old enemy until the executioner's axe put an end to Cromwell's career in 1540.

With Cromwell and Anne of Cleves out of the way, it was the turn of the Catholic party at court to make a bid for power. Norfolk began to look around for a suitable young woman who would be another—but more successful—Anne Boleyn. His choice fell on another of his nieces, Catherine, the daughter of his younger brother Lord Edmund Howard. Catherine was young and pretty; she had been brought up in the country under the rule of her old grandmother; she had no close connections at court and had not been involved in the scandals and intrigues of recent years. Also, Norfolk observed with satisfaction, she showed a pleasing willingness to follow the advice of her uncle. He summoned her to London.

The plan worked well. The king was intrigued by the Howard girl. There were boat trips on the Thames and late suppers in the royal apartments, often attended by Norfolk—cheerful, friendly, but watchful. The king was enslaved. On the very day that Cromwell was executed on Tower Hill, Henry VIII privately married his fifth wife, Catherine Howard.

While the honeymoon was still in progress, several people (including a priest) were arrested for spreading dangerous gossip about the new queen. They appeared before the Privy Council, which decided that there was nothing to make a fuss about and released the prisoners with a warning to mind their tongues. The king was not informed of this small incident, which was no doubt as unimportant as the council believed. But it was a straw in the wind.

Catherine Howard was not the innocent country girl that both Norfolk and the king believed. The household of the dowager duchess near Norwich, though mainly inhabited by women, was no nunnery. The old duchess's maids were a lively lot, and Catherine herself had received more than one whipping for being too friendly with a certain young man. In fact, she had a serious love affair in Norfolk, and after coming to London she had foolishly become involved in another with a handsome young courtier called Francis Dereham. Unwisely, Catherine did not breathe a word of this to her uncle.

After her sudden rise in the world, some of her former servants wrote asking for assistance, and Catherine took them into her household. She was thus surrounded by people who knew her dangerous secrets.

Meanwhile, the newly married couple, though they made a strange pair (Henry was old enough to be Catherine's father, almost her grandfather) seemed very happy. They made a royal progress through the north of England, where Henry hoped to win over those who had sympathised with the Pilgrimage of Grace, and were greeted everywhere by friendly crowds. Everyone could see how the king adored his pretty queen.

By the time the royal party had returned to London, the queen's days were already numbered. Information had reached Archbishop Cranmer, a leader of the Protestant party at court, of Catherine's activities in peaceful Norfolk, and a secret investigation was under way. The results were damaging and Cranmer, though fearful of Henry's reactions, volunteered to lay the facts before the king.

Hampton Court, Middlesex. At first Henry would not believe the accusations, but the evidence was overwhelming. He left the palace of Hampton Court without seeing Catherine again.

By this time Catherine knew what had happened, and she must have realised her situation was desperate. Cranmer, a kind man in his way, found her "in such lamentation and heavyness as I never saw no creature, so that it would have pitied any man's heart". The queen was sent captive to Syon House, an abbey that had been suppressed by Cromwell's commissioners. The Privy Council set about building up a case to condemn the queen, though some of the young men accused (including Francis Dereham) refused to give evidence even under torture.

Norfolk acted quickly to preserve himself. He took part in the search for evidence that would condemn Catherine, and personally discovered a trunk full of papers which, it was said, involved the old duchess in Catherine's guilty secrets. But he also decided that it would be wise to retire from court for a time, and went to Kenninghall. From there he wrote a fawning letter to King Henry. "The most abominable deeds done by two of my nieces [Anne Boleyn and Catherine Howard] hath brought me into the greatest perplexity that ever poor wretch was in," he wrote. But he hoped that the disgraceful behaviour of his relations would not turn the king against him: "I beseech Your Majesty to call to your remembrance that a great part of this matter has come to light by my declaration." And he ended: "prostrate at your royal feet, most humbly I beseech Your Majesty [to tell me] how Your Highness doth weigh your favours towards me; assuring Your Highness that unless I may know Your Majesty to continue my good and gracious lord . . . I shall never desire to live in this world longer."

Catherine Howard died on the block; the Duke of Norfolk once more succeeded in keeping his own head safely on his shoulders.

A suspected traitor on the rack— a form of torture used in Tudor times to "assist the authorities with their enquiries".

"The Sweetest Poet"

Henry Howard, the eldest son of the third duke, was created Earl of Surrey at the same time as his father succeeded to the dukedom, in 1524. He was then about seven years old. Although he is remembered chiefly as a poet, he was a courtier and soldier like his father, and he wrote most of his poetry in odd moments or when he had nothing else to do (in prison, for instance).

Surrey had more than his share of the Howards' boldness and pride, and not quite enough of the caution that kept his father safe amid the storms and troubles of Henry VIII's court. He took part in suppressing the rebels of the Pilgrimage of Grace, but returned to court soon afterwards while his father remained to pacify the north. Surrey was a sincere Catholic and strongly opposed the growing Protestant influence at court, which was represented by the Seymour family. Henry VIII's third wife was Jane Seymour. The hot-blooded young earl soon quarrelled with Edward Seymour (the future Duke of Somerset and Protector of England) and struck him. The penalty for such an act of violence at court was cutting off the right arm. Cromwell saved Surrey from that fate, but he spent several months as a prisoner in Windsor Castle.

One advantage of his imprisonment was that it gave him a chance to write poetry, and it was at Windsor that he composed some of his most attractive love poems, including the sonnet to

Windsor Castle, Berkshire.

The shield presented to Surrey by the Duke of Tuscany.

"Fair Geraldine". It is not likely that Surrey was actually in love with the "Fair Geraldine", because if (as most people think) she was in fact Lady Elizabeth Fitzgerald, she was only ten years old when Surrey wrote his poem. In the face of the pretty child, Surrey saw the beautiful woman that was to be (although, if her portrait is life-like, she did not grow up to be especially beautiful).

After his release from Windsor in 1537, Surrey went to the country where he was less likely to get into trouble; but hearing that a marriage was being planned between his sister and Sir Thomas Seymour, he came racing back to court in fury. He was damned if a Howard should marry one of "those saucy fellows that had crept into Court under their sister's [Jane Seymour's] petticoats". The Duke of Norfolk was not keen on this match either, and Sir Thomas Seymour perhaps did not care to risk a duel with the Earl of Surrey, so the idea was dropped.

The wisdom of Sir Thomas's decision was demonstrated not long afterwards at the tournament held to celebrate the marriage of Anne of Cleves, in which Surrey excelled all others with his courage and skill.

40

Surrey got rid of more of his aggressive energy after this on an expedition to France, but in 1542 he was involved in another quarrel in England. His opponent this time was John Leigh, a distant relation of the Howards, who had insulted (or so Surrey thought) the Duke of Norfolk. Surrey sent him a challenge to fight a duel, but as a result he was arrested himself and imprisoned in the Fleet prison. The duke persuaded his proud son —though with difficulty—to write a letter to the Privy Council begging their pardon for disturbing the peace, and by the time the earl was released, John Leigh had left London.

Surrey himself left the city soon after his release to join his father campaigning in Scotland, but he was already on his way back to London when Norfolk won the battle of Solway Moss in 1542. Soldiers on leave like to enjoy themselves sometimes in a rather vigorous manner, and Surrey was no exception. With some equally high-spirited friends, he was staying at a boarding house off Cheapside, where the wine was good and the company jolly. After dark, Surrey and his companions strolled through the streets, not perhaps looking for trouble, but certainly quite willing to find it. There was, of course, a riot, though not a very serious one. The houses of one or two Protestant gentlemen had their windows smashed, and a few Protestant apprentices (who may even have started the violence) were hurt by stones fired from crossbows.

Next day Surrey regretted his wild behaviour, but it was too late for regrets. The Lord Mayor of London made a formal complaint to the Privy Council. Surrey was summoned to appear before them and, once more, he found himself in the Fleet prison. He occupied himself this time in writing, not love poems, but a sharp satire on the city of London, which began:

> "London! Hast thou accused me
> Of breach of laws? The root of strife!
> Within whose breast did boil to see,
> So fervent hot, thy dissolute life. . . ."

Perhaps these verses amused the king and made him feel more kindly toward the troublesome earl. At any rate, Surrey was soon released from prison to rejoin his family in Norfolk. He was planning to build himself a mansion on Mousehold Heath, above the River Wensum with a fine view of Norwich Cathedral.

Later in the same year (1543) he went to join the army in France, and found an admirer in no less a person than the emperor Charles V, who wrote in a letter to the English king: "he [Surrey] has borne good witness in the army as to whose son he is . . . showing withal so noble a heart and such skill [in warlike arts] that he has no need to learn anything more". During an attack on a French town, Surrey was wounded and left for dead. But he was saved by his squire, Thomas Clere, who in saving the earl's life was wounded himself and died some time later.

In 1545 Surrey was in France again, this time as commander-in-chief, but to his intense anger he was superseded in his command by his old enemy, Edward Seymour, now Earl of Hertford.

An old print showing Norwich in 1558.

*Norwich Cathedral from
the south-east.*

King Henry VIII was by this time approaching the end of his life and, as his son and heir was still a child it was clear that a regent, or "Protector", would have to be appointed to rule for him. Hertford was the favourite for the post, but Surrey could not bear the thought of that upstart achieving supreme power. Moreover his father, the senior duke in England, had an obvious claim to the appointment.

Courtiers in the time of Henry VIII had to be very careful of what they said, but Surrey could never guard his tongue. He made no secret of his opinion that his father ought to be the Protector, if one were needed, and he boasted of what he would do when that day came and the Howards were the greatest family in the land. In his old age, the king had grown increasingly frightened of treason and more cruel in suppressing any sign of it, real or imagined. It did not take much to convince him that a plot was being prepared. A case of treason was constructed against the Earl of Surrey. It was a flimsy case, based on servant's gossip and on Surrey's foolish boasts. The most serious charge was that Surrey had incorporated the arms of Edward the Confessor into his own coat of arms, which showed, so his accusers said, that he was aiming at the Crown. This was nonsense: the Howards had a right to the arms of Edward the Confessor and Surrey's forbears had worn them without provoking any accusations of treason. Nevertheless, Surrey was arrested, together with his father the duke, and charged with a plot to seize the Crown.

Surrey was tried before a jury which had been carefully selected for the job and knew, before the case started, that they were expected to bring in a verdict of guilty whatever the evidence. Surrey conducted his own defence with courageous scorn for his accusers, but he knew that it was futile. He was sentenced to be hanged, drawn and quartered. The sentence was modified to simple beheading, and he was executed on Tower Hill on 21 January, 1547. The sentence was carried out in private, for Surrey —"the bravest soldier, the sweetest poet and the noblest gentleman of his time"—was a popular man, and the authorities feared a riot.

The luck of his father, the old Duke of Norfolk, still held good. In an attempt to save himself, he had actually confessed that he and his son were guilty of their non-existent "crimes". An Act of Attainder was passed against him nonetheless. (The advantage of this procedure—finding a man guilty of treason by Act of Parliament—was that awkward prisoners could be executed without a long trial, their property passed to the Crown and all their heirs were disinherited.)

The act against the duke became legal on 27 January. He would have been executed the following day—but Henry VIII died that night and Norfolk was saved. He spent the six years of Edward VI's reign in the Tower, but when the Catholic Queen Mary, came to the throne in 1553, he was released. The Act of Attainder was reversed and he was restored to all his titles. He was then about eighty years old, yet straightaway he took command of a force sent to quell a rebellion in Kent. The next year he died peacefully at his house in Kenninghall.

An execution scene on Tower Hill showing the sort of crowd the authorities were anxious to avoid for the execution of Surrey.

Mary I

A Duke between Two Queens

When the third Duke of Norfolk died in 1554, he was succeeded by his grandson Thomas, eldest son of the Earl of Surrey. The fourth duke was only eighteen years old, and he did not take much part in court life until the reign of Elizabeth, which began in 1558. But by that time the young duke was already a widower, as his first wife had died after less than a year of marriage.

Lady Mary Fitzalan

Although it did not last long, this marriage was very important for the future of the Howards. The young duke's wife was Lady Mary Fitzalan, daughter of the Earl of Arundel, and it was through her that the ancient earldom of Arundel eventually passed to the Howard family. That is why the seat of the Duke of Norfolk today is Arundel Castle, in Sussex.

Thomas Howard, the fourth duke.

47

Elizabeth I

Queen Elizabeth preferred her young male courtiers to remain unmarried, but Norfolk soon married again after the death of his first wife. Nevertheless, he remained a favourite of the queen who, besides being his sovereign, was also his cousin (her mother was Anne Boleyn, granddaughter of the second Duke of Norfolk). The fourth duke was a spirited and ambitious young man, although he lacked the craftiness of his grandfather and the force of character of his father. He spent a lot of time at court looking very splendid but not doing much. He was extremely jealous of the queen's chief favourite, Robert Dudley, Earl of Leicester, and in 1565 he quarrelled with him and foolishly struck him in the presence of Elizabeth. The queen made them put aside their quarrel, but Leicester did not forget. Norfolk made a silly mistake in turning the clever and powerful Leicester into his enemy.

It is impossible to say exactly when Norfolk first thought of marrying Mary, Queen of Scots. He kept his plans a secret, and that, too, was a mistake. It is not likely that Elizabeth would have permitted the marriage if she had been in Norfolk's confidence, but to keep the idea a secret naturally made it look highly suspicious when the facts were known. Elizabeth was not married and, as long as she had no children, Mary, Queen of Scots stood next in line to the English throne. Norfolk was therefore aiming high. Moreover, Elizabeth's ministers suspected Norfolk of being a Roman Catholic and, in Elizabethan England, Roman Catholics were looked on as potential traitors.

Mary was obviously a desirable bride for an ambitious nobleman with royal blood in his own veins, and it was certainly not love that sent the duke in pursuit of the Scots queen. By the time they first met, Norfolk had had three wives and Mary had had three husbands. All the same, she did write him some affectionate letters, beginning "My own dear lord" and ending "Yours faithfully unto death". Mary was a strange, romantic woman, and the attachment between her and Norfolk perhaps became more than the political project it was at the beginning.

In 1568 Mary fled from Scotland to England. Queen Eliza-

Mary, Queen of Scots

beth found her presence very embarrassing. For anyone who was dissatisfied with Elizabeth's government—and, for one reason or another, many people were—Mary, Queen of Scots looked like an attractive alternative. In her semi-captivity, Mary became the centre of plots and intrigue.

Norfolk's desire to marry the exiled Scots queen was still unknown to Elizabeth; but a number of English nobles encouraged his plan. Among them was the Earl of Leicester, who probably saw that Norfolk was digging a pit for himself. When Elizabeth did hear about it, she gave Norfolk a broad hint that she did not approve. It was a danger warning, and Norfolk seemed to have taken the hint. He told the Queen that his estates in England were worth nearly as much as the whole kingdom of Scotland, and he was quite content to rise no higher in the world than Duke of Norfolk. But he did not break contact with Mary, Queen of Scots.

In 1569 a rebellion broke out in the north of England; one of its objects was to release Mary. Norfolk denied that he had anything to do with it, but nevertheless he was confined to the Tower for a short time.

Two years later a new conspiracy—the Ridolfi plot—was discovered. This time there was no doubt that Norfolk was involved. A letter was produced in which he promised to send money to the rebels. He returned to the Tower under a charge of treason.

The prayer book and rosary used by Mary, Queen of Scots—now at Arundel Castle. She gave the rosary to the fourth duke.

At his trial, Norfolk admitted that he had planned to marry the Queen of Scots without Elizabeth's permission—and had continued to do so after he had promised to give up the idea. But he denied that he had plotted rebellion or encouraged the enemies of Elizabeth, and it was probably true that Norfolk had no intention of taking up arms himself against the throne. But that did not save him from the death sentence. For a long time Elizabeth could not bring herself to agree to the execution of her cousin (she suffered similar doubts over the execution of Mary, Queen of Scots sixteen years later), but her ministers insisted that Norfolk must die. He was executed on 2 June, 1572, and an Act of Attainder removed the title from his successors: there were no more Dukes of Norfolk for nearly a hundred years.

A document commemorating the death of the fourth duke.

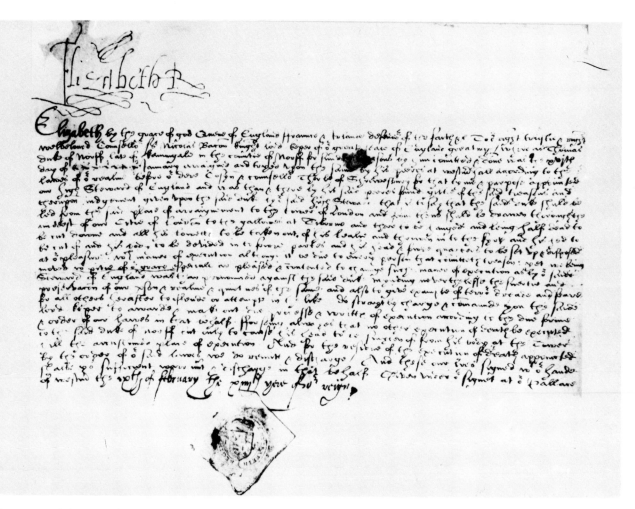

Death warrant of the fourth duke, signed
reluctantly by Queen Elizabeth I.

Howard of Effingham

Charles Howard, second Baron Howard of Effingham, was a nephew of the third Duke of Norfolk. The third duke's exploits on land as a general were matched in the days of Elizabeth by the exploits of his nephew at sea, for Charles Howard was the greatest of the sea-going Howards.

He was born in 1536 and, like his father before him, entered government service while still a young man. In 1569 he was the general of cavalry during the suppression of the northern rebellion, and in the following year he commanded a squadron at sea for the first time. He succeeded to the barony of Effingham on the death of his father in 1573, and was appointed Lord Admiral of England in 1585, when he was nearly fifty.

Tall and good-looking, Howard was an intelligent man whose gift of leadership did not exclude his taking advice from others. Although he was a very grand figure at court, especially in his later years, he was kinder and more tolerant towards ordinary people, whether they were sailors or farm workers, than most Elizabethan noblemen.

Howard became Lord Admiral at a dangerous time for England. Rivalry with Catholic Spain, especially in the West Indies where Sir Francis Drake and others raided the Spanish colonies, had been growing for several years, and in 1587 the English government learned that King Philip II of Spain was preparing a huge fleet to invade and conquer England and force the English heretics to return to the Roman Catholic faith.

In December Howard received his orders to make ready to repel the Spanish Armada, and he hoisted his admiral's flag in the *Ark Royal*. In the fleet were many captains far more experienced in naval warfare than Howard—men like Drake, his second-in-command, Hawkins and Frobisher. But in those days no commoner could lead the English fleet, and that was why Howard, rather than Drake or Hawkins, was the Lord Admiral. But Howard had enough sense to consult his subordinate officers before making decisions.

Sir Francis Drake, second in command to Howard.

Late in July the great Armada appeared in the English Channel, and the English fleet put out to meet it. For nearly a week the Spanish ships proceeded on their stately way up the Channel while the English ships hung on to their flanks, unable to break the Spaniards' defensive formation nor to do much damage to their massive wooden hulls. But as long as the Armada kept moving it was not dangerous, and Howard regarded his cautious tactics as successful. "Their force is wonderful great and strong," he reported to the government, "and yet we pluck their feathers little by little."

The main battle took place off Gravelines, but Howard missed it because he had stopped to attack a Spanish ship that had become separated from the main fleet. As the Spaniards could not gain control of the English Channel, they were forced to retire, losing many ships on their way back to Spain. The immediate danger was over and the English had won a great victory—the most famous English naval victory until Nelson beat the French at Trafalgar over two hundred years later.

Great improvements were made in the English navy in Elizabeth's reign, chiefly through the reforms of John Hawkins, the secretary of the Naval Board. Howard deserves some of the

The Spanish Armada off the English coast; the English fleet lies to the right of the picture.

The Earl of Essex

credit, for he wholeheartedly supported Hawkins against the opposition of other members of the Board. He spent part of his own fortune, which was not a large one, on the navy, and he braved the anger of the penny-pinching queen on more than one occasion by asking for better treatment for the ordinary seamen.

Although Howard was too great a figure in the kingdom to take part in the kind of raids against the Spaniards in which men like Drake excelled, he was given command of the naval side of an expedition against the Spanish port of Cadiz in 1596. The army side was commanded by the hot-headed young Earl of Essex, Queen Elizabeth's favourite, who was rather jealous of Howard. With this clumsy division of command, it is not surprising that the expedition failed to achieve any great success. Essex claimed the credit for what success it did have, and he was furious when Elizabeth made Howard Earl of Nottingham because, together with his office of Lord Admiral, this made Howard senior to Essex.

The last act of this courtly rivalry was played out four years later. Essex, that spoiled young nobleman, disgraced himself by raising a rebellion against the queen: Howard was one of the commissioners during the trial at which Essex was sentenced to death.

By the end of the reign Howard had become the most important man in England. In 1599 he was given the title of Lord Lieutenant General of All England, commander-in-chief of both the army and the navy. No other man has ever held such an office in England since. As an elderly man, Howard's name and reputation carried enormous prestige in the country, rather like the Duke of Wellington in the reign of Victoria or Winston Churchill in the years after the Second World War. He continued in favour after 1603 under the new monarch, James I. When he went as an ambassador to Spain in 1605, his progress was like that of a great monarch.

He continued to be consulted on every important government matter until 1619, when an investigation into the navy showed that it had fallen into decline. Although Howard was not blamed, he felt that he was too old to take charge of the reforms which the investigation had shown to be necessary, and he retired from his high offices. He lived another five years, his mind still clear and full of sharp good sense, and his letters still full of humorous and colourful phrases. He died in 1624 at the great age of eighty-seven.

Lord Howard of Effingham,
first Earl of Nottingham.

Earls of Arundel

St. Philip Howard

The fourth Duke of Norfolk's first wife, Lady Mary Fitzalan, lived just long enough to give birth to a son, Philip, who would have followed his father as duke but for the Act of Attainder that disinherited him in 1572. Through his mother, however, Philip Howard was heir to the ancient earldom of Arundel, and he succeeded to that title on the death of his mother's father in 1580.

As a young man he was an idle, fun-loving fellow, but when he was about twenty-four he went through a profound change of character and became a Roman Catholic. Since the Reformation of Henry VIII's reign, the heads of the Howard family have been Roman Catholics more often than not, but in Elizabeth's reign it was still a dangerous thing to be. Politics and religion were closely connected: to Elizabeth's ministers it seemed unlikely that a man could be both a loyal Catholic and a loyal Englishman. The unfortunate fourth duke had been suspected of Catholicism, though he had always denied it, and so was the young Earl of Arundel.

He wisely decided that it would be safer to live abroad, but as his ship was leaving harbour it was intercepted (Elizabeth's government had a highly efficient secret service and Arundel's plans were known long in advance). Like his father, his grandfather, and his great-grandfather before him, he entered the Tower of London under guard. "Leaving the kingdom without the Queen's permission" was a charge he could not deny, though he refused to admit a further charge that he had been associated with "enemies of the Queen".

He spent several years in the Tower until, in 1588, a further accusation was made against him: that he had prayed for the success of the Spanish Armada. He was tried and sentenced to death for treason, but the sentence was never carried out. Instead he was left to rot away in the Tower, until the horrid conditions of his prison broke down his health—though not his courage. He died in the Tower in 1595. An inscription that he wrote on the wall of his room there can still be seen. It says (in Latin): "The more affliction be endured for Christ in this world, the more glory we shall obtain with Christ in the next". In 1886 the pope bestowed upon Philip Howard the title of "Venerable" and, nearly a hundred years later, he was named as a saint. In March, 1971, his remains were moved from the Fitzalan Chapel to a shrine in the Roman Catholic cathedral high on the hill on which Arundel is built. The shrine bears the same brave words that St Philip Howard wrote on the wall of his cell in the Tower of London.

A copy of the inscription carved by St Philip Howard on the wall of his cell in the Tower.

For the rest of Elizabeth's reign, the family of Philip Howard remained in disgrace, but after James came to the throne Philip's son, Thomas Howard, succeeded to the earldoms of Arundel and Surrey.

Thomas, the young earl, was a strong character, like his ancestors, but his interests were rather different. He astonished the magnificently dressed courtiers by appearing in plain dark clothes. He was a collector of art objects, sculpture especially (the Arundel Marbles in Oxford come from his collection) and he did not care for soldiering.

Portrait by Van Dyck of Thomas, fourteenth Earl of Arundel and his wife Alethea. His interest in the exploration of the world is depicted by globe, compasses, etc.

The Arundel Marbles at the
Ashmolean Museum, Oxford.

59

Thomas, fourteenth earl of
Arundel. The Arundel
Marbles appear in the
background.

*Alethea, his wife. In the
background of both
portraits are views of
Arundel House, London.*

He did not lack ambition and, finding that his career at court was handicapped by his religion, he left the Roman Catholic Church in which he had been brought up and became a member of the Church of England. Soon afterwards, he was made a member of the Privy Council and, later, Earl Marshal.

Arundel had his share of the proud Howard temper, although in one quarrel in the House of Lords he came off second best. The Lords were discussing some business concerning ancient rights and privileges, and Arundel, in a fury, shouted at his opponent, Lord Spencer: "My lord, when these things you speak of were doing, your ancestors were keeping sheep!" Quick as a flash, Lord Spencer replied: "And yours were plotting treason!"

Arundel's rash tongue twice landed him in the Tower, and his refusal to apologise made matters worse. The vast powers of the English monarch, however, were already under attack, and kings could not so easily clap their subjects into gaol without good reason. The House of Lords threatened to "strike"—by refusing to carry on the government's business—until the Earl of Arundel was released.

When the Civil War broke out, Arundel, who did not greatly care for either side, went abroad. He never returned to England, dying in Italy in 1646.

His son and heir, Henry Frederick Howard, did fight in the Civil War on the king's side. He was with his father in Italy when he died and returned to England to take up his inheritance of Arundel. (He was also Earl, but not Duke, of Norfolk: this title had been bestowed on his father in 1644.)

Henry Frederick seems to have been an unattractive character: there was a dispute within the family over his father's will, and he treated his widowed mother unkindly. He died in 1652 at the age of forty-three, but despite his early death he left a large family: nine sons and three daughters. Two of his sons were to hold the title Duke of Norfolk, and the two others were the ancestors of later dukes.

A fifth son, Philip (1629–1694), joined a religious order

despite strong family opposition, and rose to the rank of cardinal in the Roman Catholic church. He was lucky to be out of the country at the time of the Popish Plot, when a murderous trouble-maker called Titus Oates produced absurd charges of treason against a large number of innocent English Roman Catholics (one of those who were executed as a result of Oates' accusations was William Howard, Lord Stafford, a son of Thomas, Earl of Arundel). The pope gave Philip Howard the title of "Cardinal-Protector of England", but he remained abroad for the rest of his life, dying in Rome in 1694.

TESTIS OVAT

Titus Oates; *Anagr.* Testis Ovat.

Testis ovat falsæ fruitur dum Crimine linguæ,
    Et referens Sceleris præmia Testis ovat.
Testis ovat, plorent liceat tria Regna, doloris
    Author quam Sicco lumine Testis ovat.
Testis ovat, quòd Terna perit, ruit Anglia, vires
    Quòd minuit proprias Scotia, Testis ovat.
Testis ovat lætus magnos disjungere Fratres,
    Et pulso è Patria Castore Testis ovat.
Testis ovat nocui dum pœna plectitur insons;
    Ebriu innocuo Sanguine Testis ovat.
Testis ovat; falsæ sed qualis ovatio linguæ;
    Qui quod iniquus, ovat, quam male Testis ovat.

Thus rendred.

Paid for his Crimes the Perjur'd Witness swears,
    And shews what for rewards his false Tongue dare.
Swears till three Kingdoms mourn; whilst o'er the prize
Our Witness triumphs with relentless Eyes.
Swears on till *Ireland* perish, *England* fall,
And *Scotland* in one common Funeral.
Swears still, dreadless of Hell, nor fearing Heaven,
Till the great *TORK* be from his Countrey driven.
Wrong'd Innocence by Perjur'd Witness dies,
Who drunk with guiltless Bloud still swears and lies.
Then since our Witness has this hardned face,
Let the false Wretch the Pillory disgrace.

*A broadsheet with the name
"Titus Oates" in an anagram.*

63

Arundel Castle

"Since William rose and Harold fell
There have been earls of Arundel
And earls old Arundel shall have
While rivers flow and forests wave."

So says an old verse by an unknown author.

The great castle at Arundel has been the home of the Howards for five hundred years and of the Earls of Arundel for nine hundred years, but the castle itself is even older than that. It was possibly one of the first stone castles built in England, by King Alfred in the late ninth century. There was certainly *a* castle at Arundel, though it may have been a wooden one, when William the Conqueror made himself King of England in 1066. William gave the castle to one of his Norman barons, Roger Montgomery, the first Earl of Arundel. At that time the castle probably consisted of only the great round keep. Roger strengthened the walls, which at this day are 3 metres thick in places. He also built the inner gateway of the courtyard, known as Earl Roger's Tower.

The castle did not long remain in Roger's family, and it was taken from the third earl by King Henry I after a siege in 1102. It passed through various hands until, in 1243, it was inherited by John Fitzalan, the first of his family to hold Arundel Castle (although the Fitzalans were not granted the title of earl until the time of John Fitzalan's grandson). Lady Mary Fitzalan, whose

The Keep (right) and the Bevis Tower.

(left) Aerial view of Arundel Castle and town.

James I

marriage to the fourth Duke of Norfolk united the Fitzalan and Howard families, was the daughter of the twelfth Earl of Arundel.

When St Philip Howard died in 1595, the castle became the property of the Crown, but it was restored to his son by King James I.

During the Civil War, while the Earl of Arundel was abroad adding to his fine art collection, the castle was held for the royalists. In 1643 Sir William Waller, one of the generals on the

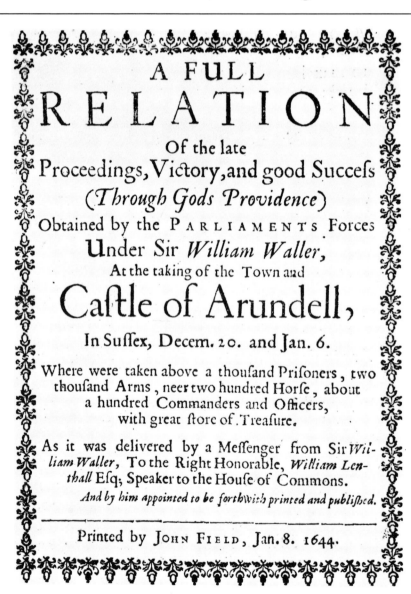

Title page of a pamphlet describing Sir William Waller's capture of Arundel Castle.

A FULL
RELATION
Of the late
Proceedings, Victory, and good Succeſs
(*Through Gods Providence*)
Obtained by the PARLIAMENTS Forces
Under Sir *William Waller*,
At the taking of the Town and
Caſtle of Arundell,
In Suſſex, Decem. 20. and Jan. 6.

Where were taken above a thouſand Priſoners, two
thouſand Arms, neer two hundred Horſe, about
a hundred Commanders and Officers,
with great ſtore of Treaſure.

As it was delivered by a Meſſenger from Sir *William Waller*, To the Right Honorable, *William Len-
thall* Eſq; Speaker to the Houſe of Commons.
And by him appointed to be forthwith printed and publiſhed.

Printed by JOHN FIELD, Jan. 8. 1644.

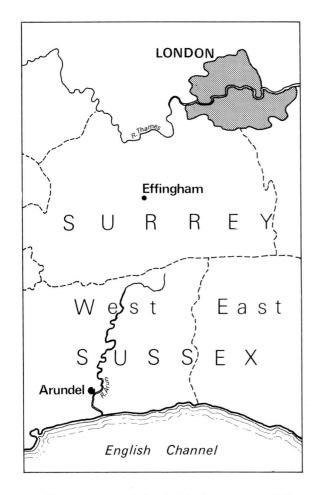

parliamentary side, laid siege to it. The castle was stoutly defended and the siege lasted for eighteen days. It might have lasted longer, but Sir William hauled his guns up the tower of St Nicholas' Church, and from there he could direct his fire downwards into the castle (the Protestant parish church actually backs on to the Catholic chapel of the Fitzalans; today they are separated only by a glass screen). Sir William also had the clever idea of draining a nearby pond, as a result of which the wells in the castle ran dry and "the Enemy began to be distressed with thirst". Reinforcements arrived for the besieging army, while the defenders, who had to release their thirsty oxen after the wells had dried up, suffered from hunger as well as thirst. The royalist commanders, Sir Edward Bishop and Sir Edward Ford, then decided to surrender, and Sir William Waller marched in. The marks made in the Barbican towers by his artillery can still be seen today.

The thirteenth century Barbican Towers (right).

Map showing Arundel in relation to London (left).

The castle was restored to its rightful owners after the Civil War, but by that time it was in a sad condition. Part of the buildings were in ruins, and many of the objects of art collected by Earl Thomas had been destroyed. The eighth and eleventh dukes restored large parts of it in the eighteenth century, but the style of architecture favoured by the eleventh duke was not very suitable for what was still basically a Norman building.

The Library, created for the eleventh duke.

An early print of Arundel

Of all its owners during the past thousand years, the castle as it stands today owes most to the fifteenth Duke of Norfolk, who carried out a large (and expensive) programme of rebuilding and restoration between 1890 and 1903. Visitors do not always realise that the great hall at Arundel, which looks so much like a baronial hall of the Middle Ages, is less than a hundred years old. In fact the whole place is more of a late-Victorian building than a Norman one, though built in medieval style. Some parts of the old castle still remain: the Keep, the Barbican Towers and Earl Roger's Tower, though much restored, are much the same as they were in the thirteenth century.

The castle was first built, on the downs above the sea, to guard against invasion (a thousand years ago, Arundel was slightly nearer the sea than it is now). During the Second World War (1939–1945) Arundel Castle was still serving the same purpose: members of the Royal Observer Corps kept watch for the enemy's approach from a look-out post high in the keep.

69

The Dukedom Restored

On the death of Henry Frederick, Earl of Arundel, his eldest son Thomas succeeded to the title. Unfortunately, Thomas was already showing signs of the mental condition that soon made him a hopeless lunatic. His brother Henry acted as head of the family, and it was largely through his efforts that the dukedom was restored to the Howards, in the person of the mad Thomas, in the first year of the reign of Charles II (1660).

The mad and wretched fifth duke died in 1677 and was succeeded by his brother. Henry Howard was something of a rough diamond. Count Grammont, a French nobleman living at the English court, described him bluntly as "a clown" and "a disagreeable person", but this judgement seems rather harsh. From other accounts, the sixth duke was pleasant enough, although rather quarrelsome, especially with his relations. As a Roman Catholic, he was active in the movement to relax the laws against his co-religionists, but his efforts were not successful. He was also interested in the newly founded Royal Society and allowed the members to meet in his London home, Arundel House, until it was pulled down a few years later. He gave his father's splendid library to the society.

In 1672 he was granted the hereditary title of Earl Marshal, and his descendants have held it ever since. But the anti-Catholic panic caused by Titus Oates made the duke decide to live abroad, in a house that he had built in Belgium. He returned to London not long before his death in 1684.

His son, also called Henry, who then became the seventh Duke of Norfolk, had gone over to the Church of England in 1679, although that was probably a "political" conversion: he did not want to follow his father into exile. At any rate, he was showered with honours by King James II, a Roman Catholic himself.

When James was overthrown in 1688 in favour of the Dutch Protestant prince, William of Orange, Norfolk at first supported

James II

The sixth duke

The seventh duke

71

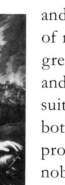

Norwich Market Place, with the church of St. Peter Mancroft.

William III

his old master. He hurried to Norwich and addressed a large meeting, advising the people to trust in Parliament to solve the problem. When it became clear that King James had few friends left in England, Norfolk announced his support for William.

Like all families, the Howards had their domestic problems, and the marriage of the seventh Duke of Norfolk provided plenty of material for those who enjoyed discussing scandal among the great. The duke's wife was a daughter of the Earl of Peterborough and, when he had married her (in 1677) it had seemed a very suitable match. As Philip, Cardinal Howard had said at the time, both the "honour and prosperity" of the family were "abundantly provided for", a polite way of saying that the bride was both noble and rich.

The duchess, however, was not so satisfied with her husband. She desired a little more excitement out of life than the duke could provide, and within a short time all London was humming with

72

gossip about the duchess's companion, a rather doubtful character called Sir John Germain, who had become rich through his good fortune at the card table. The duchess was packed off to a convent in France for a time, but when she returned to London her behaviour did not improve. The duke sued Sir John, but was awarded only a token sum of damages and, when he applied to the House of Lords for a divorce, his application was refused. Indeed, public opinion was on the side of the duchess; when the duke went to the theatre, he was loudly booed by the audience.

The scandal dragged on for several years. The duke eventually got his divorce, but died soon afterwards in 1701. The duchess then married Sir John Germain.

The seventh Duchess of Norfolk.

The End of the Senior Line

As a result, perhaps, of the failure of the seventh duke's marriage, he had no children. He had one brother, who went into exile with James II and was drowned at sea in 1689. This brother had five sons: two of them became Catholic priests and two became Dukes of Norfolk. The eldest, Thomas, succeeded as eighth duke on the death of his uncle in 1701.

The time when England was ruled by the king with the advice of his chief nobles had long since passed away, for Parliament had made itself the chief power in law and government. In the eighteenth century, dukes and earls were no longer the great men in the country that they had been two hundred years before.

The Dukes of Norfolk suffered under a particular handicap —their religion. Since the reign of Elizabeth, Roman Catholics had often been persecuted, and the overthrow of the last Stuart king in 1688 had been followed by a series of harsh laws against Roman Catholics. The government was not so much concerned with people's religious beliefs: the reason for the penal laws against Catholics was political. A Roman Catholic in the England of William III and his Hanoverian successors was suspected of being (and often was) a supporter of the exiled Stuarts, who were Catholics. When he fled to France in 1688, James II did not give up hope of regaining the throne; his son James Edward, the "Old Pretender", and his grandson "Bonnie Prince Charlie" kept the Stuart claim alive for over fifty years.

Of course, there were plenty of English Catholics who were not disloyal, yet who suffered under the penal laws. The Howards themselves were not all Catholics, but most of them were, including the eighth Duke of Norfolk. As a rule they showed the skill of their ancestors in steering a middle course between political extremes, while holding on to their ancient faith.

The eighth duke was involved in a Jacobite (pro-Stuart) plot in 1690, and his brother (later the ninth duke) was concerned in the Jacobite rebellion of 1715. He was arrested and tried for treason, but there was no evidence that he had taken part in the rebellion and, thanks to his brother's influence, he was acquitted.

It is hard to say how dangerous the Jacobite threat really was. Sir Robert Walpole and his colleagues in the government made the most of the danger in order to reinforce their own power, but there was certainly a plot of some kind afoot in 1722, when the Howard brothers were again arrested. The duke had probably given money to the Jacobites, but nothing more. He spent six months in that gloomy building which had held so many Howards in its time, the Tower of London, but there was not enough evidence to bring a serious charge against him.

It was during the time of the eighth duke that the ducal palace in Norwich was pulled down. The duke had quarrelled with the mayor and citizens of that city and had no wish to live there any more. However, a more important reason for destroying the palace, which was probably the largest private house outside London, was that it was falling down of its own accord. It had been built on low ground and the foundations had been gradually weakened by high tides, which invariably flooded the cellars.

The south side of the Duke's Palace in Norwich.

The eighth duke died without children in 1732 and was succeeded by his brother who, though only three years younger, outlived him by forty-five years.

Although the life of the ninth duke was very long, it was not very eventful. His greatest interest was in the rebuilding of his manor house at Worksop. A bad fire in 1761 destroyed much of the work, but the duke merely said "God's will be done", and began again. However, the house was never finished.

The senior line of the Howards ran directly from Sir William Howard of East Winch to the ninth duke of Norfolk. Son had inherited from father, sometimes grandson from grandfather, or occasionally brother from brother. But the ninth duke, who died in 1777 at the age of ninety-one, was the last of this direct line. Of all the sons and grandsons of Henry, the seventh duke, he was the only survivor, and on his death the title passed to another branch of the great Howard family.

The ninth duke

Norfolk House in London, built for the ninth duke, between 1747 and 1756, demolished 1938.

The Howards of Greystoke

The tenth duke

The ninth duke's successor was Charles Howard of Greystoke (or Greystock) in Cumberland, his second cousin and a great-grandson of Henry Frederick Howard, Earl of Arundel. He was brought up a Catholic and spent most of his time in his study, for he took no part in public life and preferred to live in the country. He was said to have some rather odd habits, and he wrote two or three peculiar books, including *Historical Anecdotes of Some of the Howard Family*.

Most old aristocratic families contain a fair number of eccentrics, and the tenth duke was certainly one. His son, the eleventh duke, was another, but of quite a different sort.

The eleventh duke, also called Charles, was born in 1746 and succeeded his father in 1786. He had very little education (the universities were still closed to Roman Catholics) but plenty of natural intelligence. He could express himself with great force and was powerfully built, with strong legs and shoulders. At a time when men were wearing pigtails and powder on their hair, the duke refused to do either and had his hair cut short.

But not only did the duke hate hair powder, he had an equally strong objection to soap and water. Once, he was complaining that he could find no cure for his rheumatism, and a fellow-peer inquired: "Have you tried a clean shirt?" The duke might never have washed at all, but when he got drunk his servants seized the opportunity to soap him down. Fortunately, he got drunk quite often.

The eleventh duke

The eleventh Duke of Norfolk was just that type of nobleman that the great cartoonists of the age, like James Gillray, satirized with such scorn. Indeed, the duke was a favourite subject of Gillray's. Loud, clumsy and coarse, he was not the kind of man it was easy to call "Your Grace". He looked, said someone who knew him, more like a butcher than a duke. Yet he had some good qualities.

In 1780 the city of London was torn by anti-Catholic riots (the Gordon riots) and it was at this time that the future duke renounced his Roman Catholic faith. He was not at all a religious man and, being interested in politics and fashionable society he was unwilling to give up public life (as many of his ancestors had been forced to do) for the sake of a faith he felt little for. Soon afterwards he got himself elected to Parliament, and began to pick up various political offices and honours—a lordship of the Treasury, a colonelcy in the West Yorks Militia, and so on. By the time he became duke, he had already been married twice. His first wife died after a few months and his second went mad, but, to be fair, no one has ever suggested that the duke's capacities as a husband had anything to do with these disasters.

In politics the duke was a Whig with rather liberal opinions. He was even suspected of being a republican—a strange doctrine for a hereditary nobleman—and his democratic ideas landed him in trouble more than once. He once attended a political dinner at the "Crown and Anchor", just off the Strand, in honour of Charles James Fox. Rising to his feet, the duke gave the toast: "Our sovereign's health. . . (everyone expected him to go on "His Majesty King George") "the Majesty of the People!" (Some accounts say it was Fox himself who said these words.) After this dinner, the duke lost some of his offices.

There are many other stories about the duke, related by gossips like Thomas Creevey, in whose diary the duke is usually called by the nickname "the Jockey" (the first Duke of Norfolk was also called "the Jockey").

The eleventh duke was a friend of the Prince Regent (George IV) and although they quarrelled at one time, the quarrel was patched up when the duke was an elderly man. They were both fond of eating and drinking too much, and they started the fashion

The Royal Pavilion, Brighton, built in the Oriental Style by the Prince Regent.

81

George IV (the Prince Regent)

for having an extra meal, a late dinner, at night. One evening when the duke was dining with the Prince Regent and his brothers, together with some other cronies, at the Royal Pavilion in Brighton, the Prince decided that they should drink old Norfolk under the table. Wine disappeared by the gallon into the large stomachs of the idle princes, and gradually the company thinned out. At last the Prince called for brandy, and one of his brothers filled an enormous glass for the duke. He stood up and drained it at one go; then, staring round the table, he announced that he would go home. But by the time his carriage was ready, the brandy had done its work and the chief of the Howards lay sprawled across the table. However, he managed somehow to stagger into his carriage and order the driver to Arundel. The carriage drove two or three times around the green, with the befuddled duke supposing he was on his way home. He dozed off again and woke up next morning, to his surprise, in one of the bedrooms of the Royal Pavilion.

The eleventh duke lived in splendid luxury and spent huge sums of money rebuilding and restoring Arundel Castle, and in buying books and paintings. He was very proud of his family, and it was said that anyone with the name Howard would be kindly received at Arundel.

On 15 June, 1815 (the night before the Battle of Waterloo) three hundred people attended a ball in Arundel Castle. True to his democratic principles, the duke wished to celebrate the six-hundredth anniversary of the signing of Magna Carta. It seems that he had originally intended to invite all the descendants of the first Duke of Norfolk. But when the list of guests reached the formidable total of 6,000, the duke regretfully gave up his pleasant idea.

Anyway, the ball was a great success and the celebrations, stimulated by the news of the victory of Waterloo, went on for several days. The duke, after nearly seventy years of living too well, fell ill a few weeks later and died the following December. On his deathbed, he was received back into the Roman Catholic Church.

The Glossop Line

"The Jockey" died without children and was succeeded as twelfth Duke of Norfolk by his third cousin, Bernard Edward Howard of Glossop who, like the Greystoke Howards, was descended from a son of Henry Frederick, Earl of Arundel.

The twelfth duke was fifty years old when he succeeded to the title. He had been brought up as a Roman Catholic and, unlike his predecessor, he remained loyal to his religion at the cost of giving up certain offices. Although the Dukes of Norfolk had long held the title of Earl Marshal, a Catholic was not allowed actually to exercise that office; the Catholic Earls Marshal had appointed deputies to carry out their duties. The twelfth duke appointed his brother, a Protestant. When his brother died in 1824, the duke decided that the time had come to end this rather absurd restriction, and he applied for a special Act of Parliament

The twelfth duke

that would allow him to act as Earl Marshal as well as hold the title. Though it met with fairly strong opposition, the Act was eventually passed.

Encouraged by the duke, as well as many others, public opinion was becoming more liberal towards Catholics in general. For years there had been talk about ending the restrictions, and in 1829 the Catholic Emancipation Act was passed. This allowed the duke to take his seat in the House of Lords. Soon afterwards his son, Henry Charles (later the thirteenth duke), was elected to the House of Commons, the first Roman Catholic to sit there since the Reformation.

Henry Charles succeeded to the title on the death of the twelfth duke in 1842. Unlike his father, he was not a very religious man, and in the argument over the Ecclesiastical Titles bill (1850) he took the government's side against the pope.

Although fierce feelings were aroused at the time, the row over ecclesiastical titles was a storm in a tea-cup. Since Roman

The thirteenth duke

Catholics had been freed from most restrictions by the Catholic Emancipation Act of 1829, the pope decided to organize the Catholic Church in England by appointing a number of English Catholic bishops and a Catholic archbishop of Westminster. It was perhaps a tactless thing to do: it could be regarded as an insult, if not a threat, to the established Church of England and to the supremacy of the queen. The prime minister described it as "insolent and insidious", a blow against "the spiritual independence of the nation", and he introduced the Ecclesiastical Titles bill to forbid the creation of Catholic dioceses in England. Although the bill was passed, it was never put into effect.

The thirteenth duke died a Catholic, but he allowed his son, Henry Granville, who succeeded him in 1856, to be educated as a Protestant. Henry Granville sat in the House of Commons as Lord Fitzalan, a name that had been associated with the Howards since the marriage of the fourth duke, and in 1842 he obtained a royal warrant to change his name to Fitzalan-Howard.

The two most important events in the life of the fourteenth duke both occurred as a result of his travels on the continent, where he was sent as a young man to forget his attachment to a certain Miss Pitt. In Athens he had a long and serious illness, during which he became very friendly with the family of the British ambassador, Lord Lyons, and he eventually married the ambassador's daughter. Benjamin Disraeli (the future Prime Minister) remarked when he heard of it that Howard had "escaped from the Pitt to fall into the Lyons' mouth".

The second important event happened in Paris. Through the influence of his close friend, Count Montalembert, he decided to become a Catholic. Thus the Howards returned to their ancient faith, and they have not departed from it since.

Henry Granville did not enjoy public life much, and he only took part in Parliament when he felt it was his duty to do so, usually in support of Roman Catholics. He opposed the Ecclesiastical Titles bill, to his father's annoyance, and when it was passed he resigned his seat in protest. He returned to Parliament when he succeeded his father, as a member of the House of Lords,

The fourteenth duke

but he remained more interested in private charities than in public affairs. He died in 1860 at the early age of forty-five, when his son and heir was only thirteen years old.

Henry Fitzalan-Howard, fifteenth Duke of Norfolk, continued his father's charitable work with fellow-Catholics. Not all the restrictions on Catholics had been removed by the Catholic Emancipation Act; for example, the universities still would not accept Catholics. The fifteenth duke kept in touch with the Vatican, and served as an unofficial secular head of the Roman Catholic Community in England; in 1887 Queen Victoria sent him on a special embassy to the pope. He held a minor office in the government of Lord Salisbury (1895–1900) and resigned in order to serve—at the age of fifty-three—in the Boer War. In South Africa he had a fall from his horse, injuring his hip, and thus was never exposed to enemy fire.

The fifteenth duke

87

The fifteenth duke was a strong and independent character. He did not always agree even with his fellow-Catholics. On the troubled question of Ireland, he was a unionist, although most Irish Catholics wanted Home Rule.

He took his office of Earl Marshal very seriously, and the country was fortunate to possess so dedicated a public servant to supervise the arrangements for the coronation of King Edward VII. This was a particularly complicated ceremony because, Queen Victoria having reigned for 64 years, no one could remember what had happened at the previous coronation. The duke's researches unearthed some ancient rituals in the coronation service which had been forgotten for centuries, and everything was carried out smoothly—more smoothly, in fact, than Victoria's coronation, which had been marred by some unrehearsed bungling and the spectacular tumble of one elderly nobleman down the steps leading up to the throne.

The fifteenth duke was a great benefactor and builder. He is still remembered in Sheffield, where he gave large areas of land to be used as parks and sports grounds and helped to found Sheffield University. He was responsible for the building of several Roman Catholic churches, of which the most remarkable are the huge and imposing Gothic buildings in Norwich (the duke's favourite) and Arundel. He also spent large sums on restoring Arundel Castle. The old building had not been well cared-for by his immediate predecessors: it was said that the steward used to take an umbrella on his rounds to keep off the rain that came through the roof.

After holding the dukedom for fifty-seven years, longer than any previous duke—the fifteenth duke died at the age of seventy, and was succeeded by his son.

The Roman Catholic Church of St. John in Norwich.

The Sixteenth Duke

Bernard Marmaduke, Sixteenth Duke of Norfolk, inherited the title in 1917 and, until his death in 1975, there had been only one change in over a hundred years. He continued the family traditions by generously supporting Roman Catholic charities, working for conservation (for instance, as president of the Council for the Preservation of Rural England) and as a sportsman. He was a well-known figure in that aristocratic sport, horse-racing, and had been a vice-chairman of the Turf Board, a senior steward of the Jockey Club, and the Queen's representative at Ascot. He was probably best known to the public for the many State Ceremonies he conducted as Hereditary Earl Marshal. He was responsible for the State Funerals of King George V, King George VI and also the

The Duke of Norfolk standing on Garter King at Arms' left as he read Elizabeth II's Accession Proclamation at St. James's Palace, London.

Coronations of King George VI and Queen Elizabeth II. His most significant achievement was, perhaps, his brilliant direction of the State Funeral of Sir Winston Churchill. His last great ceremonial occasion was the Investiture of the Prince of Wales in 1969 at Caernarvon Castle.

*The sixteenth duke
as a young man.*

Besides these traditional duties, the duke broke new ground in 1962 when he accepted the job of manager of the England cricket team touring Australia, showing that the descendant of an old and noble family and a man of generally conservative ideas could fit easily into the modern world. The duke married in 1937 the Hon. Lavinia Mary Strutt, daughter of the 3rd Baron Belper; they had four daughters.

The Seventeenth Duke

Having no male heirs, the sixteenth duke was succeeded by his kinsman, Miles Francis Stapleton Fitzalan-Howard, 12th Baron Beaumont and 4th Baron Howard of Glossop, a great-great-grandson of the 13th Duke. He served in the Army for thirty years, retiring as a Major-General, and during the 1939–45 War was in France, North Africa, Sicily, Italy and North West Europe.

Like most of his forebears he is a member of the Roman Catholic Church and is devoted to the unity of all Christians and other faiths. The Duke married in 1949 Anne Mary Teresa Constable Maxwell; they have two sons and three daughters.

He represented the Queen at the funeral of Pope Paul VI, the installation and the funeral of Pope John Paul I and the installation of Pope John Paul II in 1978.

The full names and titles of the seventeenth duke are: Major-General Miles Francis Stapleton Fitzalan-Howard, Companion of the Bath, Commander of the Order of the British Empire, Military Cross, Deputy Lieutenant of West Sussex, Duke of Norfolk, Earl of Arundel, Earl of Surrey, Earl of Norfolk, Baron Beaumont, Baron Maltravers, Baron Fitzalan, Clun and Oswaldestre, Baron Howard of Glossop, Earl Marshal and Chief Butler of England.

The heir to the Dukedom of Norfolk is his eldest son Edward William, Earl of Arundel.

The Seventeenth Duke with
Pope John Paul II

Index